Feeling Thankful

Written by **Shelley Rotner** and **Sheila Kelly, Ed.D.**

Photographs by **Shelley Rotner**

The Millbrook Press **M** Brookfield, Connecticut

I'm thankful for me.

For the things that I have

and the things that I do.

I'm thankful for all the people that
are special to me: my family. . .

my friends . . .

and my teachers too.

I'm thankful I have a home

and good food to eat.

I'm thankful for the
places where I play.

I'm thankful there are birds,
butterflies, flowers, and trees.

I'm thankful when I walk in the rain.

I'm thankful for the moon

and the morning, when it comes.

I'm thankful for the
whole wide world.

For Mim, Katie, and Sally.
S.M.K.

To Sheila Kelly, for whose friendship, collaboration, and inspiration I am truly thankful.
Also, special thanks to Scott Messinger.
S.R.

Library of Congress Cataloging-in-Publication Data
Rotner, Shelley.
Feeling thankful / written by Shelley Rotner and Sheila Kelly; photographs by Shelley Rotner.
p. cm.
ISBN 0-7613-1918-2 (lib. bdg.) — ISBN 0-7613-1437-7 (pbk.)
1. Gratitude—Juvenile literature. [1. Gratitude.] I. Kelly, Sheila M. II. Title.
BF575.G68 R68 2000 179'.9—dc21   00-035483

Published by The Millbrook Press, Inc.

2 Old New Milford Road

Brookfield, Connecticut 06804

www.millbrookpress.com

Printed in the United States of America.

Designed by Carolyn Eckert

LIB.   1   3   5   4   2

PBK.   1   3   5   4   2